C000177824

Nowt so dait ...2

by Kieran Meehan

Published by Meehan Cartoons

www.nowtsodaft.com

© 2014 The author retains sole copyright
to the contents of this book. All rights reserved.

ISBN 978-0-9573082-4-4

Published by Meehan Cartoons

3

6

11

15

18

23

27

28

29

31

Five years ago we offered Professor Lang unlimited resources to create the perfect deterrent. Today, I'm happy to say...
UH-OH!
Perfect
Detergent

37

Stop looking at me as if I were a piece of meat... and you were vegetarian.

39

40

41

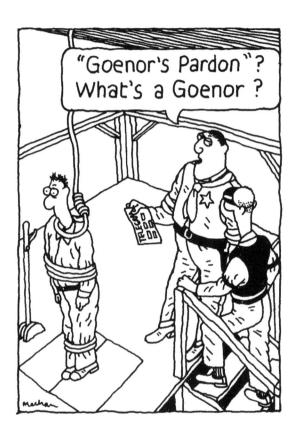

45

When I told Mrs. Mackay there was nothing I could do about the wee neds who were terrorizing her, she became very upset and said I was, "worse than useless."
At which point you arrested her?

48

49

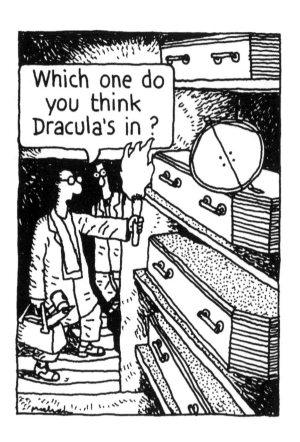

52

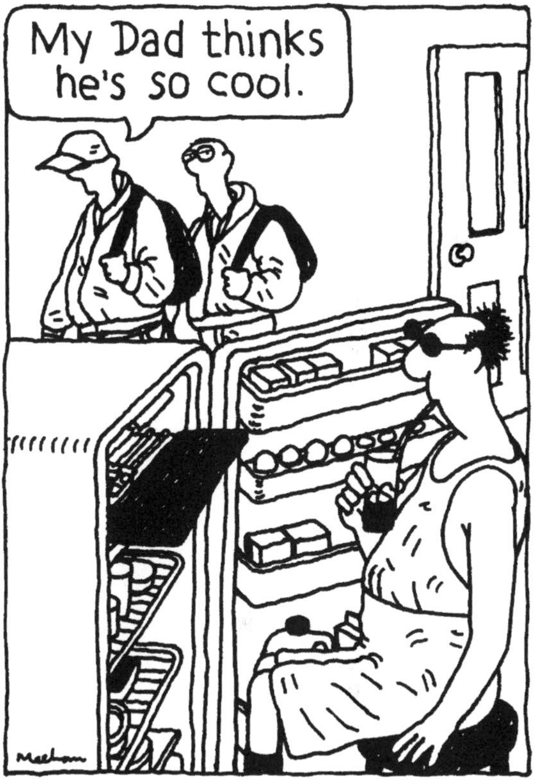
My Dad thinks he's so cool.
Macham

OK, OK! You were right and I was wrong.
TOO LATE! I've changed my mind.

61

You'll talk eventually. We just need to find the chink in your armour, your Achilles heel... YOUR blue suede shoes?
You fiend!

79

81

I know it's controversial, but my calculations prove beyond doubt that a nod is **BETTER** than a wink.
y=k=jb=i p
d=vt
d=vt
d=vt v at
Meehan

A shared sense of humour is vital for a happy relationship... As I discovered the day my wife stopped laughing.

90

94

108

110

118

120

123

125

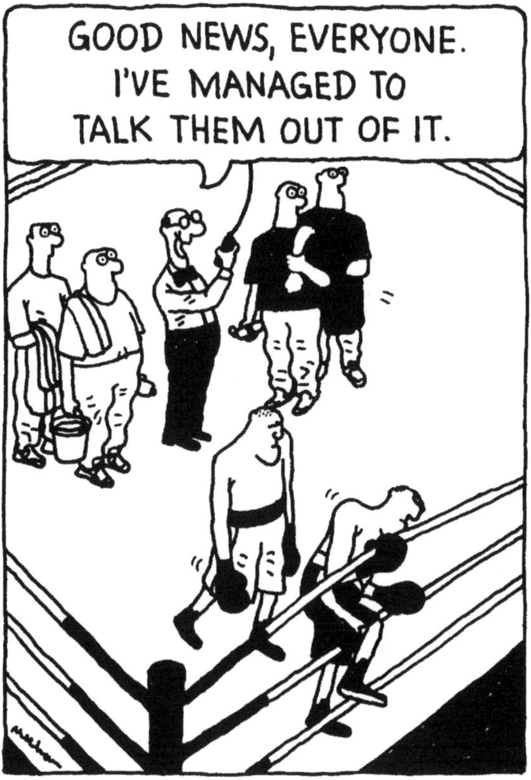
GOOD NEWS, EVERYONE.
I'VE MANAGED TO
TALK THEM OUT OF IT.

129

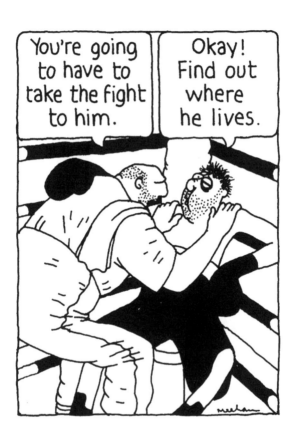

I'm a say what I say and mean what I mean kind of guy...
I mean, a say what I mean and mean what I say kind of guy.

139

147

149

Good news, Dear. The local was selling all drinks at £1.50. You will not **BELIEVE** how much money we saved.
Meehan

155

162

169

170

171

174

175

At this stage I can confirm that one person is helping the police with their enquiries.
LIC

177

181

183

189

Oh, great! We've been going round in right-angled triangles.
Meehan

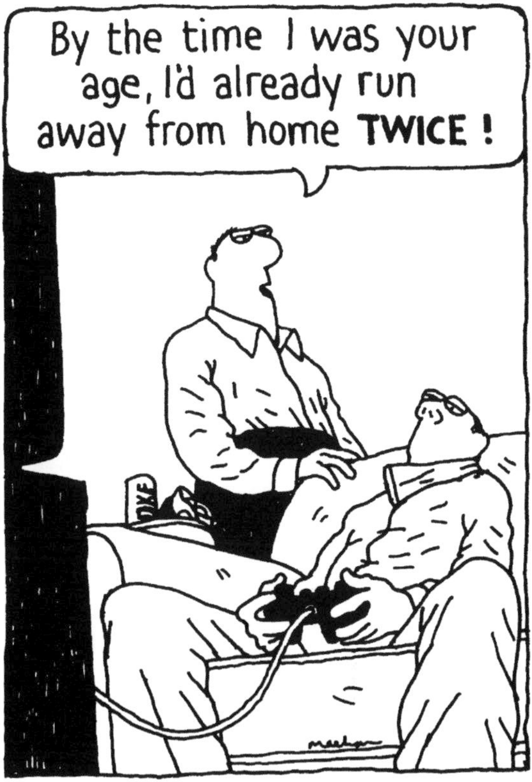
By the time I was your age, I'd already run away from home **TWICE** !

197

www.nowtsodaft.com

'Nowt so daft…' clothing, mugs, prints and other
merchandise can be purchased online at www.cafepress.com
Single panel cartoons can be purchased for reprints
and merchandise through Cartoon Stock at
www.cartoonstock.com

The Comic strip, 'Pros & Cons,' can be viewed and
purchased through King Features Syndicate at
www.Dailyink.com
and the Cartoonist Group at www.cartoonistgroup.com

© 2014 The author retains sole copyright
to the contents of this book. All rights reserved.

ISBN 978-0-9573082-4-4

Published by Meehan Cartoons

27592715R00116

Made in the USA
Charleston, SC
17 March 2014